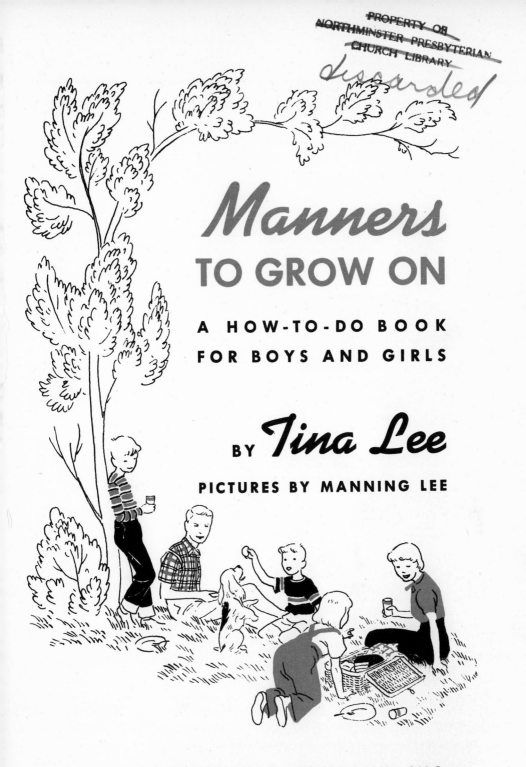

Manners
TO GROW ON

A HOW-TO-DO BOOK
FOR BOYS AND GIRLS

BY *Tina Lee*

PICTURES BY MANNING LEE

DOUBLEDAY & COMPANY, INC.
GARDEN CITY, NEW YORK

To Bucky

Printed in the U. S. A.

Copyright, © 1955, by Tina Lee

Library of Congress Catalog Card Number: 54-9846

15 14 13 12 11 10

Contents

Why Manners?

*W*hen people say that you have good manners, they generally mean that you always try to say and do things which show consideration for other people. It is important to know about good manners as you will need them every day. Having good manners is somewhat like playing a game because there are rules to follow. These rules are easy to learn, and once you know them you can start having fun with your manners. When you know that you have done something in the right way, you will feel as if you had scored a point.

Practice a little, just as you would when learning to play any game. That way good manners will soon become a part of you. When this happens, other nice things will happen too. You will find that you are making more and more friends, and because everyone enjoys having you around, you will usually be included in all the fun that goes on at home and at school. Best of all, you will be happy and relaxed, knowing that you are not likely to make any serious mistakes.

The first and most important rule of good manners is kindness and consideration of others. This rule never changes. There are styles in behavior just as there are styles in clothes and automobiles. These styles are called custom, form, or etiquette, and they change from time to time.

Customs vary in different countries, so that sometimes what we consider good manners in the United States may not be thought correct in England, France, or Japan, just as many foreign customs are not considered correct by us.

For example, in the Orient belching loudly after eating is considered a compliment to the hostess, as it's supposed to indicate how much you've enjoyed the food. This would be considered anything but good manners here at home.

In France, the knife and fork are always used when eating an apple or other large piece of fruit at the table. The fruit is held with the fork while pieces are peeled and cut off with the knife. Our simple way of biting into an apple would probably seem strange to them.

Bedouins in the Sahara Desert all eat from one large dish, dipping into it with a slice of bread. Eskimos eat long strips of meat by putting one end into their mouths, holding the other end, and slicing it off right under their nose.

When traveling abroad, you will find many things different from what you are accustomed to at home. Instead of complaining about these differences consider them part of the fun of traveling. It is interesting to see how different people do things anyway.

All boys and girls should have basic good manners. This means knowing such things as when and how to say thank you, how to write a friendly thank-you note, how to introduce friends to each other and to grownups, and to feel at home with the silver they meet at the table.

This is your very own etiquette book, planned and written especially for you. All the rules for good manners are in it, easy to read and easy to follow. Get acquainted with the index, which starts on page 94; it is your special guide when you want to learn about some particular thing. If you are having a party and would like to know exactly what is expected of you, look under "P" until you come to the word "Party." After the word you will see the number of the pages on which you will find what you should know about parties. Look under "F" for "Friends" if you are interested in knowing how to make and keep them, and under "G" for "Guest" when you are going to visit someone for a week end. Use the index often, and soon you will know and like your book as you would an old friend.

If from time to time you feel that you have made mistakes and that there are quite a few things you don't know, it needn't get you down. Everyone feels that way now and then. This is a good time to start improving your manners. With this book to help, you need never feel at a loss again.

TINA LEE
Boxwood Farm

Introductions

Do you feel tongue-tied and confused whenever you introduce a friend to a grownup or to another friend? Lots of people do, usually because they're not quite sure what to say. Introducing people to each other is not hard once you understand exactly how it's done.

THE FIRST THING to remember is to take it slowly. Never hurry through an introduction. Pause a minute to think whom you are introducing, and to whom they are being introduced.

WHEN INTRODUCING FRIENDS to each other, the boy is always presented to the girl, regardless of his age. Look at the girl as you mention her name first, then turn to the boy as you say his. "Mary, this is George Harris—Mary Smith."

WHEN INTRODUCING TWO BOYS, one of whom is much older than the other, you should introduce the younger to the older. Mention the name of the older boy first. "Bob, this is Tom Smith—Bob Jones." If they are near the same age, it doesn't matter which name you mention first. Follow the same rules when introducing two girls.

6

BOYS ALWAYS SHAKE HANDS when introduced to other boys. They shake hands with a girl, too—if she offers her hand first. But if she makes no move to offer it, a boy should just bow slightly.

GIRLS SELDOM SHAKE HANDS when introduced to other girls, but there's no rule against their doing it if they want to. Usually they just smile and say: "How do you do?" or "Hello, Mary,"—or whatever the girl's name happens to be.

WHEN INTRODUCING BOYS TO OLDER PEOPLE, always mention the name of the older person first, for example: "Aunt Frances, this is George Bland. George, this is my aunt, Mrs. Allen."

TO INTRODUCE A BOY TO EITHER OF YOUR PARENTS, the right thing to say is: "Father, this is George Bland," or "Mother, this is George Bland." Never say: "George, this is Mr. Smith," or whatever your father's name happens to be. The only time it is correct to mention your parents' last name in an introduction is when the person to whom you are introducing your mother or father does not know your last name, or when because your mother has married again her name is not the same as yours. In such cases, you should say: "Mother, this is George Bland—my mother, Mrs. Hayes."

7

WHEN INTRODUCING A GIRL TO A MAN OR A WOMAN, always say the older person's name first, such as: "Aunt Frances, this is Mary Smith—my aunt, Mrs. Allen," or, "Dad, this is Mary Smith."

IF A GIRL IS SIXTEEN OR OLDER, the man should always be introduced to her, regardless of his age. "Mary, this is my father. Dad, this is Mary Smith." If he is a person of particular importance, such as a bishop, senator, the mayor of a large city, or the President of the United States, the girl should be introduced to him. "Bishop Hopkins, this is Mary Smith."

INTRODUCE YOUR PARENTS to older people instead of the other way around. For instance, to introduce your mother to your teacher you should say: "Miss Miller, this is my mother." When introducing your father to a woman such as your teacher or a friend's mother, you should say: "Mrs. Jones, this is my father."

WHEN YOU ARE INTRODUCED, all you have to remember is to look at the person, smile, and say: "How do you do?" Never say: "Pleased to meet you," "A pleasure, I'm sure," or, "Hi!" After the introduction you don't have to say anything unless you happen to think of something especially interesting.

WHEN INTRODUCED TO A MAN, a boy shakes hands. A girl may either shake hands or smile pleasantly. If she is twelve years old or younger, she might like to make a small curtsy.

WHEN INTRODUCED TO A WOMAN, a boy shakes hands if she offers her hand first. If she does not offer it, he bows slightly as he says: "How do you do?" A girl smiles pleasantly as she shakes hands or makes a curtsy and says: "How do you do?"

THE CURTSY. For many years it has been the custom for young girls to make a curtsy when introduced to grown ups. Not a deep one, as though they were being presented at court, but just a little one, like the girl in the picture. This is one of those customs which is changing, and many people no longer consider it necessary. However, if you like to make a curtsy you should continue to do so, as it is not only polite, but very charming.

KNOWING WHEN TO INTRODUCE is as important as knowing how. When you take a friend to someone's house, always introduce him to the people you see there. If someone you meet on the street stops long enough to chat, he should be introduced to whoever may be with you. Any friend you bring home should be introduced to members of your family. Never let a person wait around while you chat on and on to someone he doesn't know.

DON'T INTRODUCE people who meet very briefy, such as the person who stops you just long enough to say a cheery hello, or the one coming out of church, a store, the movies, or a large building when you and a friend are going in.

Your Friends

$\mathcal{F}$riends are important because without them there would be no one with whom to play, work, talk about plans, ideas, hopes, or troubles. It's nice to share these things, especially with someone who understands how you feel.

THE SUREST WAY TO MAKE FRIENDS is to remember that friends don't just happen. You must be the sort of person that people are glad to have around. Do your part in making others want you as a friend, and the best way to make others like you is for you to like them first.

AN IMPORTANT RULE in making and keeping friends is never to say or do anything which might hurt them. Having friends is largely a matter of having people like you. Most people will like you if you are considerate of their feelings.

SHOW INTEREST IN YOUR FRIENDS and in the things they like and do. Listen attentively to the things they may want to tell you. Offer suggestions when your opinion is asked. Be careful not to overdo the interest to the point of asking such questions as, "How much money does your father make?" or, "Are your parents divorced?" Be understanding and interested in any personal details which friends may tell you, but always let such information come from them.

DON'T JUDGE A FRIEND by how much or how little he has. The sort of person he is and whether or not you enjoy being together are the things that matter.

COMPLIMENTS are always nice to hear. If you think a friend does something especially well, don't hesitate to tell him so. If Albert draws well, you might say, "Albert, you're a mighty good artist," or, "I wish I could draw like you." Albert will be very pleased.

WHEN SOMEONE PAYS YOU A COMPLIMENT, such as, "You look so pretty in that dress," or, "I love the way you sing," all you need to do is smile and say, "Thank you." Never make remarks about what's wrong with your voice or your dress.

EVERYONE IS DIFFERENT from everyone else. In fact, no two people in the whole

"I WON THE GAME!"

"I HAVEN'T SEEN
YOUR OLD DOLL."

world are exactly the same. So if someone you meet is lame, blind, wears strange clothes, or has trouble speaking, remember that these differences are only more noticeable than most. Treat these people just the way you'd like to be treated. Remember that their feelings are no different from yours. Don't stare at them and never ask questions such as, "What's the matter with your tongue?" or, "How did you get blind?" Questions like these are embarrassing and unkind.

PUTTING YOURSELF IN A FRIEND'S PLACE is one of the first things you should learn, and here's how to begin. Imagine how it would feel to be one of the different people just mentioned and it will help you to understand how they feel. Once you understand, you will be sympathetic, and when you can sympathize with a person, you're on the way to knowing how to put yourself in his place.

NEXT TRY TO IMAGINE how a friend feels when he loses a pet or has some other disappointing experience. Imagine how you'd feel if it had happened to you. Do this often, and soon you'll get into the habit of putting yourself into a friend's place. Soon you will find that without thinking about it you are understanding, sympathetic, and helpful. You will discover that not only do people seem to like you but how much you like them, too.

12

THE SHOW-OFF breaks all rules of friendship and isn't very popular. Usually he is only trying to make himself liked by telling everyone about what he imagines are his good points. He doesn't seem to know that his show-off ways only annoy and hurt others. The show-off usually speaks louder than anyone else and does everything to attract attention. He likes to brag, and his favorite subject is himself. Girls show off and brag too, and they are as annoying as a boy show-off once they get started on the subject of themselves. So don't be a show-off.

STICK TO THE TRUTH if you want your friends to like and trust you. And did you know that unless you can be trusted you aren't much of a friend? You may think it funny to make up a story about someone or to say a few things which aren't true, in an effort to make yourself more interesting. But such things aren't funny and often can lead to trouble for your friends and for you.

WANDERING FROM THE TRUTH can easily become a habit, and when this happens, your friends know it almost before you do. After that, they'll find it hard to believe you, even when what you're saying is really true.

MISTAKES ARE MADE by everybody, and often these mistakes get us into trouble. When this happens to you, don't make up an untruth in the hope of escaping blame. Be truthful. Admit what you've done, explain how it happened, and say: "I am really very sorry." Most people will admire your courage and truthfulness.

"I'M SORRY. I DID IT."

"SHE DID IT."

BLAMING SOMEONE for something you have done is not fair, so promise yourself right now that you'll never do it. Have the courage to admit your mistakes. You'll be glad you did.

NEVER BLAME OTHERS, even when you're sure that they're guilty. Give them a chance to admit what they have done themselves. You'll avoid being thought a tattle-tale.

BAD-TEMPERED PEOPLE who act up when something goes wrong or when they can't have their own way are no fun at all, are they? In playing and living with others it's pretty important to keep your temper under control. Remember that no one can have his way all the time, especially in group activities, where what to do is often decided by a vote. So be pleasant when things don't go to suit you.

MOODS, both good and blue, are something we all have, but don't let your blue ones spoil your fun or your friendships. Never sulk when in a mood. It is better to stay to yourself if you think you might be unpleasant. Read a book, watch TV, listen to the radio, or work on a hobby. A blue mood soon passes, and then you can emerge your cheerful self again, ready to enjoy your friends and have them enjoy you.

BORROWING has spoiled many a friendship. Avoid it whenever you can. But should you find it necessary to borrow something, remember that what you borrow is usually considered precious by its owner. Treat it more carefully than if it were your own. Return it promptly and in good condition, and don't forget to say: "Thank you for letting me use it."

14

How to Be a Good Sport

A good sport is a person who is always fair in all his dealings with others and who is cheerful when things go wrong or when he can't have his own way. He knows how to take the bad as well as the good with a smile. Everyone finds him pleasant to have around. Good sportsmanship should extend beyond games into everyday behavior at school, at home, or wherever you happen to be.

JOIN CHEERFULLY IN WHATEVER IS GOING ON in the way of games or other activities, and be good-natured when things don't suit you.

YOU'RE NOT ALONE if you find it hard to be a good sport. Lots of people have the same trouble, but you can learn sportsmanship just as you can learn anything else.

PLAYING GAMES is one of the best ways to learn about good sportsmanship. Remember that games are supposed to be fun, so try your best to win. If you lose, don't

"MY LEG HURTS."

"THE SUN'S IN MY EYES."

"YOU PUSHED ME."

spoil the game for others by sulking, and remember that winning isn't the only thing that matters. If winning is really important to you, practice to improve your game. Try a little harder when you play—you'll win before long.

BE FAIR ABOUT SCORING. Be sure a point is yours before you take it. Should there be any question as to who won a point, let the other player have it. Never take advantage of younger friends because you're bigger or stronger than they are.

NEVER SULK when you are losing a game. No one will believe or respect you if you make excuses such as, "My leg hurts," or, "The sun's in my eyes," or, "You pushed me just when I was going to hit the ball."

BE PLEASANT WHEN SOMEONE ELSE WINS. This may seem very hard when first you try it because it is natural to feel disappointed at not winning yourself, but after some practice you'll get the hang of it. One day you'll surprise yourself by feeling really glad for the person who wins. When this happens, you'll know that you're a good sport.

16

"I'M GLAD YOU WON."

Conversation

Speech is a very important part of life and manners as it is the best means by which people can express their thoughts and ideas to others. Have you ever noticed that the way something is said can indicate your mood? When two or more people are speaking together, it is called conversation. This chatting together can be fun and lively when the subject talked about is something interesting to everyone. What is said by one person often makes another think of something enjoyable to add.

Being a good listener is as important as having something to say because when you listen with interest it encourages others to talk.

WHEN YOU'RE INTRODUCED to someone, you know that "How do you do?" is all that you have to say. Most grownups will ask you a question or say something which will start conversation rolling.

WHEN ASKED A QUESTION, the first thing to remember is to answer it promptly. Avoid getting into a long story which eventually leads to the answer after everyone has got tired of listening. Answer the question first, and then go on with whatever it was you wanted to say.

ANSWER PROMPTLY.

DON'T GO ON AND ON

"NO, MRS. JONES."

DON'T BE SHY

"ARE YOUR PARENTS DIVORCED?"

AN ABRUPT "YES" OR "NO" is not a polite way to answer questions. Always add a person's name, such as, "Yes, Mrs. Smith," or, "No, Mrs. Jones."

SPEAK UP PLEASANTLY when someone speaks to you. Smile and show some interest in what is being said. It's not always easy to pop up with something amusing, but by listening attentively you'll often get an idea for an interesting incident to talk about.

SHYNESS WITH STRANGERS often keeps us from pleasant conversation. This is usually because we don't think they'd be interested in what we have to say. This feeling can be overcome to a great extent by acting as if you had known these strangers for a long time, and talking to them as if they were your best friends. Try it.

ASK QUESTIONS if you want to spark conversation. When a friend has been away, ask about where he or she stayed, what he saw and did. Then sit back and listen. If a friend is interested in dogs or horses, ask a few questions about them. You'll find that as they talk the conversation will sparkle because people like to talk about the things which interest them.

PERSONAL QUESTIONS are those which pry into a person's private affairs or into his family's finances, or any question which you think a person would rather not answer. Avoid such questions as, "Why doesn't your sister like your aunt Sue?" or, "Was your uncle Bill fired from his job again?" or, "Your father doesn't give your mother very much spending money, does he?" Would you like to have someone ask you such questions?

TABLE TALK should be about pleasant things. Don't get talking about gory details of an accident or illness. Avoid the things which might spoil others' appetites.

FAMILY DINNER CONVERSATION can be very pleasant because as a rule everyone is more relaxed and less hurried than at other meals during the day. The talk should be directed to different members of the family. Movies you've seen, books you've read, happenings of the day, and things you've heard are all pleasant to tell about. Don't shout across the table to a person at the other end, and be careful not to interrupt when someone is talking.

WHEN VISITING IN A FRIEND'S HOUSE, speak pleasantly with members of the family or any of their friends you may meet there. Avoid unpleasant remarks about people or things in a friend's house.

SAYING "NO" is hard when a friend asks you something you'd rather not do. Put yourself in a friend's place and say "No" the way you'd like to have it said to you. An abrupt "No" is very rude. If you say "I'm sorry" when you have to refuse, it will be easier all around. Say: "I'm sorry, but I can't go," "I'm sorry that I can't let you wear my ring, because I couldn't get another if it should be lost," "I'm sorry, but Mother doesn't want me to lend my raincoat." These are all ways of saying a kind and polite "No" and doing it so other people won't feel hurt.

NEVER WHISPER to one person in the presence of someone else. It is not considerate because it makes the one who can't hear feel left out. He might even think you're saying something unpleasant about him.

DON'T TALK ABOUT
UNPLEASANT THINGS

WHEN VISITING
BE AGREEABLE

NEVER WHISPER

Gifts and Giving

*T*here seems to be a magical quality about giving which somehow makes the giver very happy. Try sharing something with your family or a friend and see how happy you'll feel.

The important part about giving is not the cost of the gift, but the fact that you have thought of someone and wanted to do something for him.

SPECIAL GIFTS are those we give to our family and friends at Christmas time, birthdays, and other festive occasions. These should be selected with special care. They need not be expensive to show that you've given them your best thought. Try to select gifts you think the person getting them will like. For instance, don't give Aunt Mary a knitting bag if she doesn't knit, or an eyeglass case to a friend who doesn't wear glasses. You get the idea.

UNUSUAL GIFTS which you can give to your family are such things as offering to wash the dishes every evening for a week, taking care of the baby some Saturday morning, helping Dad wash the car, or weeding the garden. Presents like these cost no money and make a big hit with the family.

A HOSTESS GIFT is one you give to a friend's mother when you have spent a week end or longer in a friend's house. It may be taken with you at the time of the visit, or sent by mail after you get back home. This gift need not be expensive, as it is not intended in any way to repay your hostess for what she has done for you, but rather, it's a way of showing your appreciation.

GIFTS WHICH COME TO YOU should be accepted with interest and enthusiasm—even those which aren't what you want. If you show that a gift displeases you, it will hurt the giver, who no doubt had hoped to make you happy. After all, the gift is never as important as the thought behind it.

NOT LIKE THIS

"THANK YOU" is the first thing to say when accepting a gift. After that, say something in your own words which will show how pleased you are. Anything which shows your pleasure and appreciation is the right thing to say.

WHEN YOU ARE ASKED what you'd like to have as a gift, don't let it be a signal to ask for the most expensive thing you can think of. It is nice to mention three or four things you'd like, but always be sure that at least one of them is quite inexpensive.

BUT LIKE THIS

A THANK-YOU NOTE is not necessary when someone gives you a present in person, as a warm thank you when you accept it is enough. But when a gift is sent you and the person is not there to be thanked, you should write a note within a few days. Keep the note short, but make it warm and friendly. All you need to know about writing thank-you notes can be found on pages 23, 24 and 25.

Letters

THIS IS BETTER   **THAN THIS**

DATE HERE

OR HERE

*I*f you like to get letters, make a habit of writing to your friends often, for writing letters means getting letters. Make your letters fun to read by keeping them cheerful and newsy.

HAVING THE RIGHT MATERIALS is the first step in good letter writing. You need clean and neat paper, with or without rules, a pen or pencils, ink, a blotter, and stamps.

USE PEN AND INK if you are able to handle them without accidents. However, a neat letter written in pencil is better than a spotty one written in ink.

HANDWRITING should be your best. Not only does it make your letters look like something special, but it makes them easy to read.

THE DATE should always be written either at the upper right corner of the note paper, or at the lower left corner of the last page of your letter.

EVERY LETTER IS STARTED with some sort of greeting, such as, "Dear Miss Jones," "Dear Mother," "Dear Johnnie." This is called the salutation of the letter. Starting a letter without a salutation is not only incorrect, it is discourteous.

AFTER THE SALUTATION comes the letter itself, and this part is called the body. Think of things to write that will make your letter fun to read. Things you've done or seen and news that the reader would like to know are all good letter ideas. Write them down just the way you'd say them, because the best letters are those which are natural.

A NICE ENDING is needed for every letter, and this is called the close. "Sincerely yours," "Yours truly," "Fondly," "Affectionately," and "With love" are all correct closing expressions. Which one you use depends upon the kind of letter you are writing and how well you know the person to whom it is going.

THANK-YOU NOTES are expected from you almost as soon as you are able to write. They should be written after you have spent one night or more in a friend's house, when someone has sent you a present, or has done something especially nice for you. Remember that you are expressing your thanks for a kindness, so keep the note short, cheery, and to the point. Never mention anything which might be wrong with a gift or anything which might have been unpleasant about a visit. This note, written by a young girl to a friend who has sent her a box of glazed fruit for Christmas, is very thoughtless.

January 3, 1956.

Dear Mrs Smith—
Thanks for the candy. It really isn't candy at all but just fruit covered with syrup. It isn't my favorite kind, but my brother is crazy about it. He ate most of it, which kept him out of the kind I do like, so everything was all right.
your friend,
Mollie

Mollie might have written either of these
notes and spared Mrs. Smith's feelings:

December 30, 1955.

Dear Mrs. Smith—
The box of candied fruit was
a wonderful surprise. I had never
had any before. Micky was so crazy
about it that he could have eaten it
all! It was so nice of you to
send it to me.
We had a very jolly
Christmas, with all the family home.
I hope yours was nice too.
Sincerely,
Mollie

Dear Mrs Smith —
Thanks so much for the
lovely box of glazed fruit. It was
sweet of you to send it. The
whole family was home for Christmas,
and we had some of the fruit after
dinner.
I hope you had a nice
Christmas, and that the new year
will be a happy one.
Sincerely,
Mollie

A letter thanking a friend's mother for a seashore week-end visit could be something like this:

June 3, 1956

Dear Mrs. Jones —
Now that I'm back home my visit with you and Mary seems like a wonderful dream. Everything was perfect, and I enjoyed it all. The mornings on the beach and the swimming were things to remember. Mother says that I've gained weight, and I'm sure it's true, after such delicious food.
Thanks so much for everything you and Mary did to make the week end so delightful.
affectionately,
Mollie

ALWAYS MENTION anything that was special about a visit or a gift. Don't be afraid to write nice and complimentary things. These notes should be written within a week—and the sooner, the better.

BE THOUGHTFUL of your friends by sending a greeting card or a cheerful note to a friend who is sick. When there is a death in a friend's family, write a short note of condolence. All that you need to say is that you're sorry and want to express your sympathy. It need not be more than this:

Dear Joan:

We've just heard the news of your father's death. It made me very sad, as I liked him so much. This is just to tell you how sorry I am and to express my sincere sympathy.

Affectionately,

Edith

Such letters take very little effort on your part but mean so much to the friends who get them.

ANSWER YOUR MAIL PROMPTLY, especially if the writer is waiting for an answer to a question. Thank-you notes which you receive do not require an answer.

KEEP A DIARY as an aid to letter writing. Refer to it when you need ideas for interesting news.

NEVER INCLUDE GOSSIP or unpleasant subjects. When there's sad news to report, don't dwell on it any longer than necessary.

A LETTER WRITTEN IN ANGER should never be sent at once. Keep it for a cooling-off period, then read it over. Unless it's the sort of letter you'd like to get from a friend, drop it in the wastebasket instead of the mailbox.

ADDRESS YOUR ENVELOPES in a clear hand and be sure that the name and address are complete and correct. Write your own name and address on the back of the envelope. This insures your letter's being returned to you, should it go astray.

POST CARDS are very handy for writing short messages or for sending to friends when you're on a trip. They shouldn't be used for personal messages, as they are open for everyone to read. Don't use them for thank-you notes, either.

ENOUGH POSTAGE should be attached to a letter or a package, as it is not considerate to have the person to whom you sent it pay for any postage you've neglected. When in doubt about proper weight or postage, have a clerk in the post office weigh your package or letter.

Invitations

*M*ost invitations are very informal. Notes, printed cards with blank spaces for the time and date, and invitations by telephone are the ones most used. Of course, formal invitations are used for weddings, engagements, and debut parties, but these will not be a part of your life for quite some time.

TO ACCEPT AN INVITATION means to say yes.

TO DECLINE AN INVITATION means to say no. An invitation should be accepted or declined as soon as possible. To say, "I'll let you know later," and then wait several days is very inconsiderate, as the person writing you cannot make plans. Your answer should be given by phone or note, according to how the invitation was given you.

TO INVITE A FRIEND TO DINNER all you need to do is to phone and say, "Can you come to dinner with us on Friday night?" If he accepts, you should say something to show your pleasure, such as, "I'm so glad. The dinner will be at seven o'clock," or whatever time your meal is to be.

INVITE A FRIEND FOR A WEEK END OR LONGER exactly as you would for dinner. If the friend lives in another town, the invitation should be by note. You might write a note like this one:

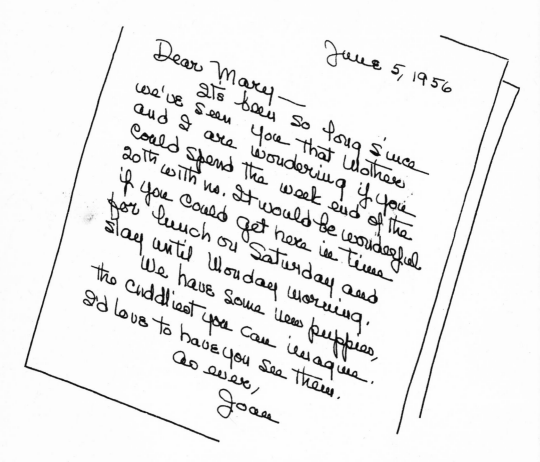

The same sort of letter may be used when inviting someone for a longer visit. These notes should be natural, warm, and friendly, so that they will make the friend getting them feel that you are really very eager to have him come to visit you.

PLANS for these visits should always be checked with your mother, and the time you choose should be one which is convenient for her.

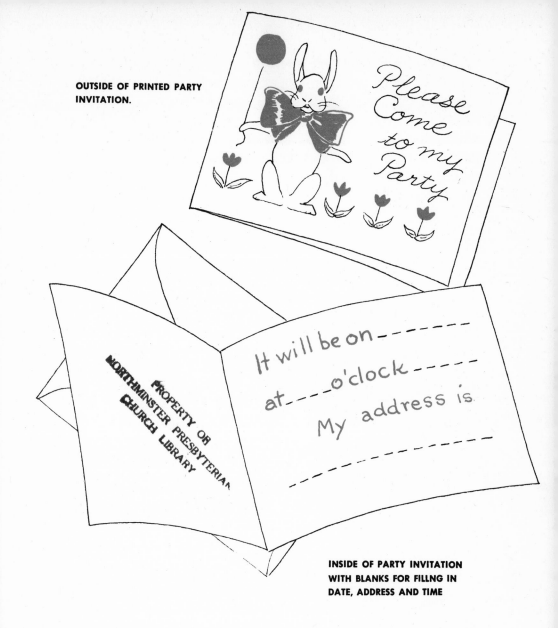

OUTSIDE OF PRINTED PARTY INVITATION.

Please Come to my Party

It will be on _ _ _ _ _ _
at _ _ _ _ o'clock _ _ _ _
My address is _ _ _ _ _ _ _
_ _ _ _ _ _ _ _ _ _ _ _

INSIDE OF PARTY INVITATION WITH BLANKS FOR FILLNG IN DATE, ADDRESS AND TIME

YOUR MOTHER should write a note or make a phone call to your friend's mother to confirm all your invitations.

PARTY INVITATIONS can be made by phone, a printed invitation something like the one shown here, or a note like the one on the next page.

REMEMBER that the best notes are those which you write in your own words because they are the most natural.

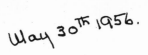

May 30th 1956.

Dear John —
Can you come to my birthday party on Tuesday the Twelfth of June, from 2:30 to 5:00 P.M. We are going to swim, so be sure to bring your bathing trunks. I hope you can come.
As ever,
Bob Smith

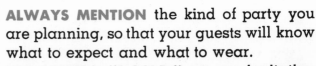

ALWAYS MENTION the kind of party you are planning, so that your guests will know what to expect and what to wear.

THE LETTERS "R.S.V.P." on an invitation mean that an answer is expected. These four letters stand for the French words, "Répondez, s'il vous plaît," which mean, "Please answer."

How to Enjoy Your Home

You probably know at least one or two boys or girls who are pleasant and fun with friends and strangers but who are sulky, rude, and demanding when at home. They excuse it by saying: "I want friends and strangers to like me, but why bother with manners at home when all I want is to be myself?" It is clear to see that good manners have not become a part of them.

BEING YOURSELF IS FINE if that self is a pleasant one, but if it's selfish, rude, and troublesome, it's time for improvements.

HOME SHOULD BE A HAPPY PLACE, and it can be if everyone does his part.

BE CHEERFUL about doing work around the house. Act promptly when asked to help. Be as pleasant to the members of your family as you are to your friends.

NOT THIS

BUT THIS

31

BE A GOOD SPORT and polish up your sense of humor if you want to get the most out of sharing a house with others. Don't sulk when you're not allowed to do something, or when you're faced with an unpleasant chore. Accepting these things along with the fun is all part of a happy home life.

GROWNUPS HAVE FEELINGS TOO, so be fair and kind in your treatment of them. Never make mean remarks about their looks or the things they do. Don't tease, annoy, or make fun of them.

MOTHERS AND DADS, in fact all grownups, get tired just as you do. And when they are tired, they may be annoyed about things which aren't really important. Sometimes they get very cross. Some days your mother may be very cheerful about things you do and noises you make, and other times she may seem cross about nothing at all. All mothers aren't this way, but if yours is, you may be sure that it's because she is very tired. Remember that her crossness has nothing to do with the way she feels about you, for she loves you as much when she's cross as when she's gay. Be especially nice to her if you think she's tired. Ask if there's anything you can do to help. You'll notice that she probably won't be cross.

DON'T EXPECT YOUR MOTHER to pick up after you or to keep track of what you do with your things. That's your responsibility, and the sooner you learn to accept it, the easier things will be all around.

FOSTER PARENTS are men and women who take care of children who have no homes of their own. They do many things to make your life pleasant. They take the place of your real parents while you live in their house. Show your appreciation by treating them as if they were your own people.

MAIDS who work in your house cleaning, ironing, or cooking should be treated with the same good manners you show toward the rest of your family.

THE BABY SITTER is a special kind of person. Sometimes she's not grown-up at all, and some sitters are men or boys. Remember that a sitter takes your mother's place. If you feel that a sitter in the house offers a good chance to do exactly as you like and that it's fun to be troublesome, you're missing what might be a very pleasant time. And of course you're being a poor sport. Be cheerful and helpful—give your manners a workout and you'll find that you and the sitter can have a good time together.

SHOW A NEW SITTER around the house and where things are kept. Play games together, or you read to the sitter instead of asking her to read to you.

IT'S A GOOD IDEA TO LISTEN when grown-ups offer advice. Remember that they've had a great deal of experience and that you can learn many interesting and unexpected things from them.

Brothers and Sisters

You're lucky if you have brothers or sisters because you can usually be sure of having someone around with whom to play games or work on projects. Model-making, raising pets, painting pictures, or playing musical instruments are all things that you can enjoy doing with your brothers and sisters.

ACT TOWARD THEM as you would toward friends. Be considerate of their feelings and careful of their property. Avoid teasing or bullying the younger ones. Be thoughtful, helpful, and kind—and see how much fun you'll have together.

BIG SISTER'S DATES are very important to her, and the young man who comes to see her or take her out should be treated as nicely as any other guest who comes to the house. When you open the door for one of her dates, ask him to come in, take his hat and coat, show him into the living room, and ask him to sit down. Unless you know him very well, you shouldn't stand around and talk, but just say: "Excuse me. I'll tell Mary you're here." Then leave the room and stay out of it. Of course, don't forget to tell your sister that he's waiting.

YOUR OLDER BROTHER'S FRIENDS should be treated the way you'd like him to treat yours. Let them have the house pretty much to themselves unless they have asked you to join them. As a rule, the things they do wouldn't interest you anyway, so busy yourself with a project of your own or play with your own friends, and stay out of brother's way.

YOUNGER CHILDREN in the house are people, too, so treat them as you'd like your big brothers and sisters to treat you.

IF A BROTHER (or a sister) tells you something in confidence, it means that he trusts you with something he doesn't want anyone else to know. So guard his secret, no matter how much you might want to tell it to someone else.

BORROWING even from brothers and sisters, is something you should do sparingly—and never without asking permission. Treat borrowed things as if they were your own best. Return them promptly and in good condition. Shirts, handkerchiefs, or cotton dresses should always be washed and ironed, scarves pressed and returned, ready to use. Don't forget to say: "Thank you."

LENDING should be done cheerfully when a brother or sister needs something you have. Be generous instead of selfish with your things.

ACCIDENTS to borrowed things should be put to rights by the person who borrowed them, even though it may mean spending time and money. If the accident happens to something which you have lent, be pleasant and reassuring about it instead of making an unpleasant fuss.

Friends in Your House

*E*veryone you invite to your house, either to play in the afternoon or to spend several weeks, is your special guest. It is up to you to do everything you can to make the visit pleasant.

YOUR FRIENDS are your responsibility, so don't expect your mother or other members of the family to entertain them. Of course, your mother will be glad to help you in many ways, especially in deciding on things to do.

PLAY IN YOUR OWN ROOM or out of doors instead of in the room where grownups are working, reading, listening to the radio, or entertaining their own friends. If you must share the room with other members of the family, play quiet games. Never turn on the radio or TV set without their permission, and don't dip into their conversation.

CHECK WITH YOUR MOTHER before you ask a friend to stay for a meal. There are times when it is not convenient to have unexpected guests.

SHARE YOUR THINGS WILLINGLY with a guest. If you have something very special which you are afraid might be broken, it is better to put it away before your friend arrives rather than refuse to let him play with it. As a rule, if you are careful of other people's things, they will be careful of yours.

THE ICE BOX is the cook's very special little island. Whether the cook is your mother or someone hired to do the cooking, all the food is in her care until it is cooked and served. So raiding the ice box and eating anything you see can sometimes lead to trouble. The poor cook is at her wit's end when the food which has been planned for a dinner is eaten by raiders in the middle of the afternoon. You'd better check with the cook before you raid. Usually she'll be glad to tell you what you can eat without spoiling her meal plans.

FRIENDS WHO VISIT YOU over night or longer are called house guests. It's your place to see that they have a nice time while they are staying with you.

GREET A HOUSE GUEST with a warm welcome. "I'm so glad you could come" is one way to make a guest feel happy and at home right away.

SHOW YOUR GUEST the room he will have while with you, and help him with his luggage. Leave him alone for a while in case he'd like to change his clothes or get his bags unpacked.

IF YOU SHARE YOUR ROOM with your guest, clean out part of your closet so that he can have a place to hang his clothes. Empty one of your bureau drawers, too. Once you've given your friend these spaces, keep your things out of them. Let your guest use the best things in the room and always give him first choice.

AT MEAL TIME, share your guest with everyone at the table by making the conversation general instead of talking only to him. Never whisper to each other or giggle together at table when others don't know at what you are giggling. Ask your guest a few questions to ease him into the conversation. Mothers are usually very helpful in making young guests feel at home too.

ALWAYS PASS THINGS TO YOUR GUEST before serving yourself. Never make remarks about your guest's table manners, or about how much or how little he eats. If he fails to wait for you to ask to be excused, but leaves the table at the end of the meal without a word, you should excuse yourself and go with him.

CANDY WHICH COMES IN A BOX or a bag should be offered to your guest directly from the box or bag, letting him make his selection. Never take a piece out of the container and hand it to him.

NEVER GO OFF BY YOURSELF, leaving your guest alone. And you'd better not accept invitations from other friends unless your house guest is included.

DON'T BE DISCOURAGED OR ANGRY if a house guest gets cross, loses his temper, or otherwise misbehaves. Of course, he has forgotten his manners, but that's no excuse for you to forget yours. Once the unpleasantness is over, treat him as if nothing had happened. No doubt he feels embarrassed at having behaved so badly and will appreciate your seeming not to notice.

GOOD-BY should be short and cheerful. When your guest is ready to leave, you should be with him, making the visit pleasant to the end. Be sure to say something cheerful, such as, "I'm so glad that you came, and I had a swell time."

The Telephone

*I*f you like to answer the telephone, make yourself popular by doing it well. Speaking clearly and being patient are the important points in easy telephone manners.

HOW TO ANSWER THE PHONE. When the phone rings, lift the receiver off the hook and wait a second to make sure that it has stopped ringing. Then say "hello" clearly and give your full attention to what the person on the phone is saying.

WHEN THE CALL IS FOR SOMEONE who is at home, say clearly, "Just a minute, please." Then find the person who's wanted—but don't call by shouting, "Hey Mom!" or, "Da-aad! Tel-uh-phone!"

WHEN THE CALL for someone who is not at home, say clearly, "I'm sorry, but she is not at home. May I have her call you later, or may I take a message?"

WHEN YOUR NUMBER IS CALLED BY MISTAKE, don't show annoyance with the person calling. It probably wasn't his fault. Say something like, "I'm sorry, but I think you have the wrong number—this is 2273," or whatever your number happens to be. This is the nicest thing to do.

"SORRY, YOU HAVE THE WRONG NUMBER."

MAKE LISTENING EASY for anyone using the phone in your house. If the radio is on, tune it very low or turn it off altogether until the conversation is over. Avoid all needless noise—and don't talk to the person who is busy on the phone unless you have something to say which simply can not wait. There are mighty few things that important.

WHEN YOU MAKE A PHONE CALL, be sure that you know the right number before you start the call. Writing it down on a piece of paper for easy reference is a good idea. Keep your mind on the number you are dialing. Speak clearly if you're giving the number to an operator.

LET THE NUMBER YOU ARE CALLING RING at least eight or ten times before you hang up. It may not be possible for the person you're calling to answer the first ring, so here's where your patience comes in handy.

WHEN SOMEONE ANSWERS THE NUMBER YOU'RE CALLING, ask at once for the person to whom you wish to speak. "May I speak to Mary Smith, please?" The person answering will say something like, "Just a minute, please," or, "I'm sorry, but Mary isn't here."

PHONE HOG

DON'T BE IMPATIENT

DON'T HANG UP ABRUPTLY when the person you're calling isn't in. Give your name and say, "I'll call again later, thank you," or, "Will you please have her call me when she comes in? My number is Elmwood 3-7572."

WHEN YOU'RE GIVEN THE WRONG NUMBER, don't be impatient with the person who answers. Remember that it wasn't his fault, and that it hasn't been pleasant for him to answer the phone for a wrong number. "I'm sorry" is what you should say, even though it might not have been your fault.

YOUR PHONE CALLS. The phone is not a toy, so please don't treat it as if it were. Calling people to play tricks or guessing games isn't really funny, and it can be very annoying to the person called.

DON'T BE A "PHONE HOG." Remember that there are other people in the house who may want to use the phone, and that someone may be trying to reach your family with an important call. Keep your calls brief.

BE A CAREFUL HANGER UPPER. See that the wire doesn't tangle between the cradle and the speaking piece, as it is in the picture. When this happens, it keeps the line open and anyone trying to reach your house will get the busy signal.

DON'T TALK
TOO LONG

DON'T LISTEN IN

WHEN SEVERAL PEOPLE in different houses use the same phone lines, it is called a party line. Either two or four families can share the same line. Party-line phones are less expensive than private wires, so they are quite popular. However, it takes consideration and patience to use a party line pleasantly.

BE EXTRA CAREFUL when using a party line. Remember that you're sharing it with others and that it really belongs to everyone. Don't talk too long. Never listen in when one of the other parties is talking—and don't talk when someone else is trying to make a call. When a party line is in use, you'll hear voices, so let that be your signal to hang up quietly. Never make rude or impatient remarks to the person using the line no matter how anxious you might be to make a call.

HANG UP QUIETLY
WHEN OTHERS ARE
TALKING

DON'T BE RUDE.
WAIT YOUR TURN

The Door

When the bell rings, do you race to the door and skid to a stop just in time to yank it open, only to find that you're so out of breath that you can scarcely speak to the person waiting outside? Try walking for a change. Open the door gently and see what a difference it makes.

WHEN THE CALLER IS A FRIEND, the doctor, a neighbor, or anyone else you know, be quick to ask him into the living room. Offer him a chair and say: "Excuse me." Then go and call the person who's wanted.

TRADESMEN, such as the milkman, laundryman, or others who come to the door on household business do not expect to be asked inside. In very bad weather, it is considerate to ask them to step inside the door.

A STRANGER AT THE DOOR should be asked politely, "What can I do for you?" When he's told you his business, ask him to wait while you call your mother or dad. Do not invite strangers into your house. Let whoever is in charge decide what should be done about them.

WHEN YOU RING A DOORBELL, press it firmly but don't keep your finger on it too long. Give the person in the house time to get to the door before you ring a second time. Make the second ring as gentle as the first. If the second ring gets no answer, try some not too loud knocking. The bell could be broken.

NEVER PUSH YOUR WAY into a house the instant the door is opened. Take it easy. Wait until you're asked in.

DON'T DASH AWAY without saying a word if the person you wanted to see is not at home. Give your name and say "Thank you" as you leave.

APARTMENT MANNERS. If you live in an apartment, remember that you share the building with other families. Don't leave your bike, skates, or other toys in the hall or on the front steps in everyone's way. Be considerate of other people by not playing loud games or jumping and singing in the hallways or on the stairs. The stairs and elevators are not the places for game playing at all. Try being quiet while entering or leaving your apartment building.

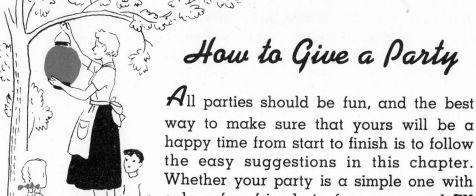

How to Give a Party

All parties should be fun, and the best way to make sure that yours will be a happy time from start to finish is to follow the easy suggestions in this chapter. Whether your party is a simple one with only a few friends in for games and TV watching, or a real bang-up birthday party with all the trimmings, its success depends upon planning and doing a few things, step by step, the right way.

MAKING PLANS WITH MOTHER is the best start for any party. Since your mother usually does most of the work, she is the one to decide what kind of party it should be, how many guests to invite, and when to have the party.

YOU CAN HAVE FUN getting together with your mother on all details, such as what games to play, whom to invite, and what the prizes and refreshments will be. Decide all these things early.

THIS IS THE TIME to tell your mother that you want to help with the work. Let her tell you what things you can do—and be sure that you do each cheerfully and well. You'll enjoy your party more if you've taken an important part in the preparations.

THE GUEST LIST should be prepared with care. Never ask more people than you can entertain with ease. When possible, each person invited should know at least one of the other guests. The best parties are those where all the guests know each other, because everyone feels that he is with old friends. School groups, your Sunday-school class, or the girls or boys with whom you have been at camp all make good party guests. There may be times when you will want to invite a friend who doesn't know any of your other friends. When this happens, see that he is introduced to everyone. Pay special attention to him until he gets used to things and is having a good time.

THE INVITATIONS are ready to be sent once you've finished your guest list. A written invitation avoids all mistakes about time and place and is for that reason better than a telephone invitation. For more about invitations see page 27.

THE HOST OR HOSTESS. A boy or man giving a party is called a host. A girl or woman giving a party is a hostess. The right kind of a host or hostess must be cheerful, happy, and jolly, making friends feel welcome and glad to be at the party. The success of your party depends upon your being a considerate host or hostess. Think of your guests instead of yourself and do the thoughtful things which make the party fun for everyone.

GREETING YOUR GUESTS CHEERFULLY is part of being a good host or hostess. Be ready—and somewhere near the door—to greet them as they arrive. "Hello, Mary. I'm so glad to see you," or, "I'm so glad you could come," are both pleasant greetings.

YOUR MOTHER or some other grownup should be near the door with you. If she does not know the guests, this is the time to introduce them. Remember about introductions on page 6. When a guest is wearing a coat, tell him where he may leave it.

PARTY GAMES should be fun for all, so plan the kind in which everyone can take part. Join in the games at your own party, and play as well as you can. But if you should win, you do not keep the prize. The reason is that you are having the game for your friends' enjoyment and the prizes are for them too. It has long been the custom for the winning host or hostess to give the prize to the second-place player.

REFRESHMENTS can be anything from cookies and milk to a complete lunch or supper, depending upon the kind of party you are giving. You should decide in advance exactly what they will be, and how you want to serve them. There are two nice ways to serve party food:

1. Setting places at one large or at several small tables, having the food served to the guests. When food is served this way, it is fun to mark the places with cards on which are written the names of the different guests.

2. Arranging the food on a large table. Napkins, plates, and silverware are also placed on the table. Guests help themselves and then find places to sit, usually in groups. This way of serving party food is usually called buffet. Be sure that all the guests are served before you start eating.

ACCIDENTS often happen at parties. So if one of your friends should spill ice cream or cocoa on your mother's best carpet or on your best dress, don't scold or look horrified. It's your place to make your guest feel that it was an accident which couldn't have been helped. Put yourself in a guest's place, be reassuring by saying something like, "It's all right, I'm sure it can be fixed."

48

Anything which makes your friend feel better is the right thing to say. The important thing to remember is to make your guest feel comfortable about what has happened.

PRESENTS are often brought to you, especially if it is your birthday. These are usually given you when the guest arrives. "Thank you" should be said at once. You may either open the gifts right away or save them to be opened at some special time during the party, when everyone can enjoy the fun of watching you open them. A second "Thank you" should be said as you open each gift. Show interest and pleasure in each one, even when it's something you don't find thrilling.

SAYING A FRIENDLY GOOD-BY is as important as greeting a friend with a warm welcome. Be on hand as each guest is ready to leave. Never wander away with one of your friends, leaving the good-bys to your mother. Your attention belongs to your guests from the time they arrive to the time they're on their way home.

"SO GLAD YOU CAME," is what you can say when a friend tells you that he's had a good time. "I had fun too," is another easy thing to say. What you say should be natural and in your own words. Make good-bys cheery and brief.

WHEN THE PARTY IS OVER, don't collapse in a chair and leave all the cleaning up for someone else to do. Be ready and willing to do your share of straightening up and dish washing. And this is the best time to tell your mother how much you enjoyed the party. "Thank you for everything, Mother, it was wonderful," will make her very happy.

49

Table Manners

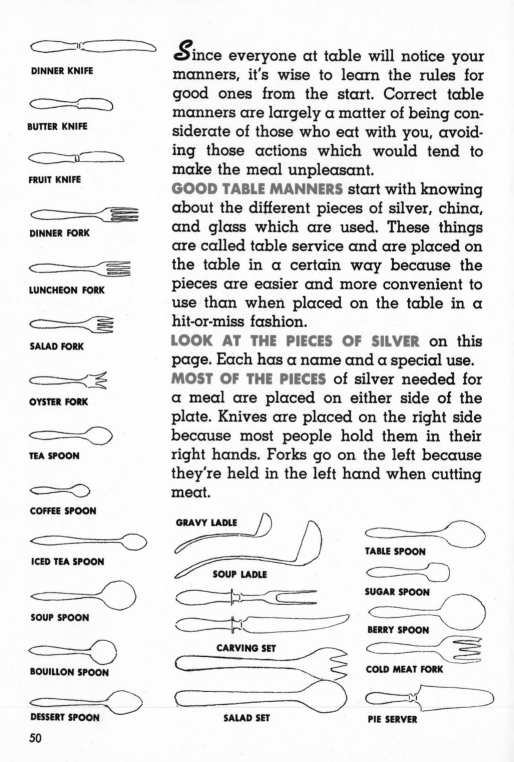

DINNER KNIFE

BUTTER KNIFE

FRUIT KNIFE

DINNER FORK

LUNCHEON FORK

SALAD FORK

OYSTER FORK

TEA SPOON

COFFEE SPOON

ICED TEA SPOON

SOUP SPOON

BOUILLON SPOON

DESSERT SPOON

GRAVY LADLE

SOUP LADLE

CARVING SET

SALAD SET

TABLE SPOON

SUGAR SPOON

BERRY SPOON

COLD MEAT FORK

PIE SERVER

*S*ince everyone at table will notice your manners, it's wise to learn the rules for good ones from the start. Correct table manners are largely a matter of being considerate of those who eat with you, avoiding those actions which would tend to make the meal unpleasant.

GOOD TABLE MANNERS start with knowing about the different pieces of silver, china, and glass which are used. These things are called table service and are placed on the table in a certain way because the pieces are easier and more convenient to use than when placed on the table in a hit-or-miss fashion.

LOOK AT THE PIECES OF SILVER on this page. Each has a name and a special use.

MOST OF THE PIECES of silver needed for a meal are placed on either side of the plate. Knives are placed on the right side because most people hold them in their right hands. Forks go on the left because they're held in the left hand when cutting meat.

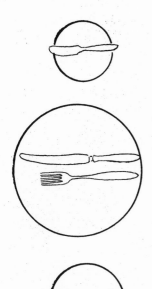

STUDY THE DIAGRAM for placing silver. Start eating with the piece of silver farthest from your plate. When the first course is soup, use the spoon farthest from your plate on the right. Follow this rule of starting from the outside and working in toward your plate, and if the table has been correctly set, you'll find that the right piece of silver is in the right place when you need it.

WHEN IN DOUBT, watch to see which piece your hostess uses. You should never start eating before she does, anyway.

WHEN YOU'VE FINISHED, your butter knife belongs across your butter plate, your salad fork across the salad plate. Your dinner knife and fork belong together on your dinner plate.

WATER TUMBLER   WATER GOBLET   WINE   PARFAIT

ICED TEA

YOU SHOULD KNOW about the pieces of china shown on these pages. After looking at the pictures, you'll know what they're for when you see them on a table.

ALL THE GLASS PIECES have their special uses too. There are many more than those shown here, but most of them will not be part of your life until you're a grownup.

NAPKINS come in various sizes; large ones for dinner, smaller ones for breakfast or lunch.

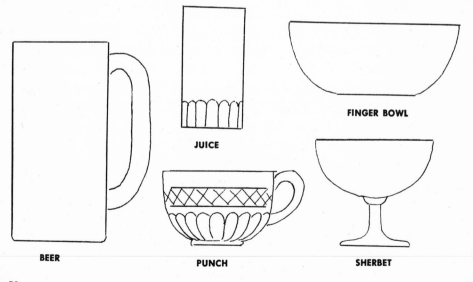

BEER   JUICE   FINGER BOWL   PUNCH   SHERBET

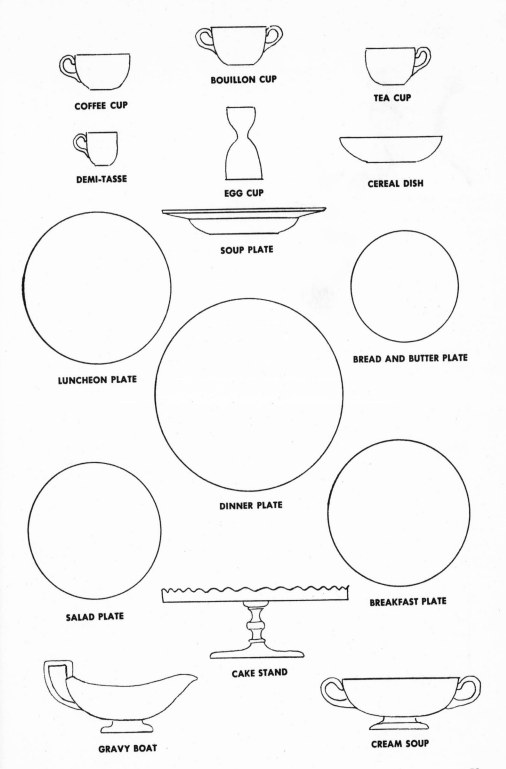

COFFEE CUP

BOUILLON CUP

TEA CUP

DEMI-TASSE

EGG CUP

CEREAL DISH

SOUP PLATE

LUNCHEON PLATE

BREAD AND BUTTER PLATE

DINNER PLATE

SALAD PLATE

BREAKFAST PLATE

CAKE STAND

GRAVY BOAT

CREAM SOUP

THE FIRST RULE of good table manners is to go to the table as soon as you're called or the meal is announced. Don't suddenly decide that you'd better get washed up, or that you want to finish playing a game or reading a story—it's rude to keep everyone waiting. It's just as rude to rush to the table, sit down, and start eating bread and butter, or whatever happens to be in sight, before everyone else is seated.

MAKE YOURSELF EASY TO LOOK AT. Brushed hair, a clean dress or shirt, washed hands and face will do the trick.

THE MEN usually seat the women in the family. When your father's away, it should be nice for you to know how to hold the chair for your mother. Here's how it's done: Stand behind the chair and draw it out far enough for her to get between it and the table. Now, watch carefully—and when she bends her knees to sit, push the chair forward gently, so that it will be there to sit on. A little practice will make your technique perfect.

WHEN YOU'RE A GUEST at a friend's house, always wait for your host or hostess to tell you where to sit. Wait until the older people are seated before you sit down.

PLACE CARDS are often used at parties, and then it's easy to find the place marked with your name.

WHEN A BLESSING IS ASKED before a meal, you should listen quietly, with your head lowered slightly. Wait until after the blessing to take your napkin from its place. Watch when your hostess takes hers if you're in doubt.

UNFOLD THE NAPKIN to half its size if it's a large one, all the way if it's small. It belongs on your lap, except when you use it to wipe your mouth. Pat—don't rub—your mouth with the napkin. Always do this before you take a drink to keep food off the edge of the glass. And don't take a drink when there's food in your mouth.

WHEN EATING SOUP, spoon it away from you—and take the soup into your mouth from the side of the spoon, never from the point. Soup is usually coolest on the top, so start spooning it from there. Never blow on soup, or stir it around in an effort to cool it.

SOUP SERVED IN A CUP should be drunk from the cup, not eaten by spoonfuls. Any solid should be eaten with a spoon.

SIP YOUR SOUP QUIETLY and never let it drip from the back of the spoon. When you've finished, place the spoon on the saucer on which the cup is resting—don't leave it in the cup.

LIKE THIS

NOT LIKE THIS

MEAT OR FISH AND VEGETABLES are served after the soup, and these are called the main or second course. This food is usually served by someone at the head of the table and plates are passed from person to person until everyone has been served. Sometimes the serving dishes are passed around the table and each person helps himself to what he wants. Often plates are served in the kitchen and one put at each place.

WHEN A MAID SERVES A MEAL, she passes all the food. She stands at your left and offers you the food from a serving dish. You help yourself to what you want, putting it on your own plate. Take the piece or pieces of food nearest you. Don't push the food around looking for some special pieces.

IT IS NOT NECESSARY to say "Thank you" to a maid who passes you food. The reason is that if each person said "Thank you" each time something was passed to him it would be distracting from the conversation. Talking to a maid while she's serving should be avoided for the same reason. Of course, you should answer any of her questions politely.

THE CORRECT WAY TO HOLD your knife and fork while cutting meat is shown in the picture. Notice that the fork is held in the left hand, with the prongs pointing down, and that the index finger is on the shank of the fork, pointing toward the prongs. The thumb is on the other side of

the fork, and the other fingers are close under it.

THE KNIFE is held in the right hand, by the handle, with the index finger pointing down the back of the blade. Hold the meat in place with the fork and cut it with the knife. Cut only one or two pieces at a time, eat these, and then cut more. Carry them to your mouth with the fork, still held in your left hand.

EAT VEGETABLES WITH THE FORK held like a tiny shovel. Don't spear vegetables. Fill the fork only halfway up the prongs. More food than this overcrowds your mouth. Always swallow the food already in your mouth before taking more. Take food from the point of your fork, never from the side.

SALAD is served on a plate of its own, either at the same time as the meat and vegetables or as a separate course. When served with the meat course, eat it as if it were another vegetable.

IF NO SALAD FORK IS PROVIDED, eat the salad with your dinner fork. Never transfer bits of salad to your dinner plate, but eat it from the plate on which it is served. Do not cut salad with your dinner knife.

BAKED POTATOES should be eaten right from the jackets, not scooped out and emptied onto the plate. If the potato has not already been scored and partly opened, do this first. Add salt and a piece of butter to the open potato. Don't stir the whole thing into a gooey mess, but mix the butter through the potato, a bit at a time, as you eat it.

EAT GRAPEFRUIT OR FRUIT CUP when served as a first course exactly as if it were dessert. And remember, don't squeeze the grapefruit rind to get the last drop of juice.

TOMATO OR OTHER JUICES should be taken by degrees, never swallowed at one gulp. Hold the glass in one hand only, and please keep your elbows off the table.

AN ARTICHOKE should be eaten by removing one leaf at a time, dipping it into the sauce provided and eating the soft part from the end as shown in the pictures. When all the leaves have been removed, scoop out the spiny center and eat the solid part of the artichoke with your fork as you would any other vegetable.

ASPARAGUS should be cut into sections with the side of the fork and eaten like any other vegetable. Remember to eat as you cut instead of cutting it all at one time. When the lower ends of asparagus are tough, it may be eaten by holding the tough part in your fingers and eating the soft part.

SPAGHETTI can be cut with the fork as you eat it, or rolled on the fork, as shown in the picture. It is often eaten this way in Italy. Roll only a small amount; otherwise, your mouth will be too full.

BREAD AND BUTTER are easy to eat when you break pieces from the slice and butter them instead of buttering a whole slice and taking bites from it. Rolls and biscuits should be eaten the same way.

YOUR FINGERS should not touch the food on your plate. If necessary, you may use a small piece of bread to help get certain pieces of food onto your fork. But unless you can do this without attracting too much attention, it is better to leave the bit of food on your plate.

SOME FOODS which may be eaten with your fingers are: olives, pickles, radishes, corn on the cob, artichokes, small cakes, bread, rolls, and fried chicken at a picnic.

WHEN A SECOND HELPING is offered, take it if you are still hungry, but don't ask for more food when you're a guest. When you pass your plate for a second helping, the silver you have been using should be on the plate and not on the table near your place.

AT HOME, when you have finished a meal, you may ask to be excused. When you're a guest, you must wait for your hostess to excuse you.

FINGER BOWLS are not used often as they once were since their use is one of the customs which is changing. But you should know what to do with one when it is put before you. Finger bowls are usually brought to the table just before the dessert is served. Each bowl is about half filled with water and placed on a dessert plate, with a doily under the bowl. One of these is put before each person.

DIP YOUR FINGERS INTO THE BOWL and then wipe them on the napkin. Now lift the finger bowl and the doily from the plate and put them on the table in front of you, a little to the left of your place. The bowl should rest on the doily, as in the picture. Now the dessert plate is ready for the dessert when it is passed. In restaurants, the finger bowls are usually brought on at the end of the meal. In this case, leave the bowl on the plate after you have dipped your fingers.

YOUR NAPKIN should be put neatly at the left of your place when the meal is over. Don't fold it unless you know you will be using it again. Different houses have different rules about napkins, so when visiting, watch what your hostess does with hers.

A LIST OF DON'TS is printed here, not because you need such a long one, for by now you probably know about most of the things mentioned on it, but to show you at a glance what you should improve upon to make your table manners high score.

Don't! Don't! Don't!

Don't lick the silver or clean it on your napkin.
Don't play with your bread as if it were modeling clay.
Don't roll your napkin into a ball. Leave it on your lap.
Don't push your plate back when you've finished. It should remain where it is until taken away.
Never say: "I'm through." Put your knife and fork across the plate and everyone will know you've finished.
Never clean your teeth by running your tongue around them while at table. It is ugly to see.
Don't lick your fingers, or wipe them on a chair seat or on the under-side of the table. Use your napkin.
Never leave the table in a fit of anger.
Don't talk so much that it interferes with your eating, or keeps others from taking part in the conversation.
Don't interrupt others.
Never be so slow or so talkative that everyone is kept waiting while you finish your food.
But—don't eat as though you were trying to win a race.
Don't drink the juice from the bottom of a dessert cup. Use your spoon.
Never pile food on the back of your fork, or put your knife in your mouth.
Don't lick bits of butter or jelly from your butter knife.
Don't chew with your mouth open, or talk while it is full.

Things Which Belong to Everyone

Do you find it easy to share the radio, TV, pets, and things which seem to belong to everyone in the family? Sharing is half the fun of living with others, but to do it easily takes good-natured planning.

GET TOGETHER with the rest of the family to make plans for how much and when the radio and TV sets may be used. Decide in advance which programs you want. Each member of the family should be allowed a few choices.

EVERYONE WILL HAVE TO GIVE A LITTLE unless there are several sets in the house, but in the end, everyone will be satisfied. Once the plan is complete, stick to it. Don't whine and beg to listen to something when it's not your time to choose.

PLANS FOR TRIPS in the family car should be made in advance too. Be a good sport about going on the bus or streetcar when someone else in the family needs the car, or if no one has the time to drive you.

RECORD PLAYERS should be used with care. Make sure it's agreeable with others before you fill the air with loud music. If the player is in your own room, you should be able to play it without disturbing anyone, especially if you turn it down or close the door.

PETS are pleasant to have if everyone will share in their care. They need to be fed, kept clean, and well cared for. They need a clean bed where they can rest. Their coats should never be matted or dirty, and they need fresh water every day in a bowl that's easy for them to use. When they're sick, they should be taken to a veterinarian, just as any other member of the family would go to a doctor. These animal doctors know through experience exactly what to do to make sick pets feel better in a short time and they are not expensive. It is risky to try to cure pets yourself. Do your share of this work gladly. If it seems too much trouble, then you shouldn't have pets.

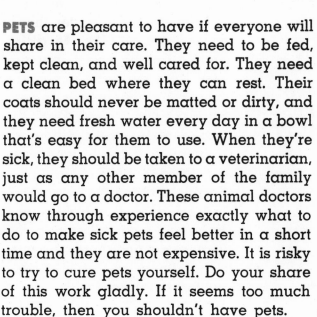

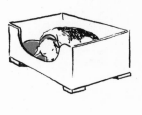

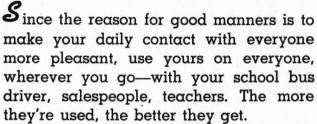

On the Street

$\mathcal{S}$ince the reason for good manners is to make your daily contact with everyone more pleasant, use yours on everyone, wherever you go—with your school bus driver, salespeople, teachers. The more they're used, the better they get.

YOU WILL OFTEN SEE different-looking people on the street, but no matter how keen your curiosity, never stare at them as they approach, or turn to get a better look after they've passed. Don't make nasty remarks about their differences, either to them or to someone with you.

STRANGERS WHO SPEAK to you are usually harmless. Often they want to ask directions, or exchange a few pleasant remarks. Unfortunately not all strangers are so innocent, and since there's no way of knowing about them, be on the safe side by not getting too friendly.

NEVER ACCEPT CANDY, ice cream cones, or auto rides from strangers. If they are offered, just say, "No, thank you," and be on your way. Should a stranger insist on walking with you, be pleasant, but never take suggestions about short cuts to where you're going. Don't take walks with them, either.

WHEN YOU'RE ON THE STREET after school, avoid crossing streets against the lights, walking too close to the curb, and leaning against shop windows with sticky hands while admiring the things inside. All these things are bad manners because they are inconsiderate of others.

WHEN WITH FRIENDS, walk, don't run, to the nearest drug store for that after-school soda. When it's crowded and you have to wait for a place at the soda fountain, do it good-naturedly, without making remarks about the slowness of the people ahead of you.

DON'T WALK BACKWARD. It usually leads you into an innocent by-stander—or something breakable.

IT MAY BE FUN to link arms with several friends and act like a tank rolling down the sidewalk, but break up the solid front when you see someone coming so that he can pass. Remember that the sidewalk is for everyone to use.

DON'T SKIN TOO CLOSE to people when you're skating or riding your bike on the sidewalk. Give them a signal that you're coming in plenty of time for them to move instead of waiting until you're right behind them. To sound a horn immediately behind someone is startling and rude.

TALKING AND LAUGHING is part of having fun, but when it is overdone it attracts the wrong kind of attention to you. It can be very annoying to those around you, too, so take it easy.

"EXCUSE ME" is the thing to say when you accidentally collide with someone, step in front of him without meaning to, or do anything which might be annoying.

*T*he rules for good behavior are the same for riding on all these forms of public transportation. The main thing to remember is that you are sharing with others who have paid their fare and are entitled to a pleasant ride. Be a good sport about whatever happens, and be considerate of those around you.

GETTING ON THE SCHOOL BUS after classes seems to be the signal for tossing manners out the window. It's natural to feel thrilled because school's out and you're free for the rest of the day, but don't let these high spirits get the better of you.

HAVE A GOOD TIME on the school bus. Tell jokes and stories, sing, play guessing games—but don't push each other around, yell, or tease schoolmates just because they can't leave the bus until they're near home.

THE BUS DRIVER is a very important person, because your safety depends upon his skill in driving. To tease him, hang around his neck, or crowd around him is not only bad manners, it's dangerous as well.

WHEN USING A PUBLIC BUS, have your fare ready before the bus comes. This will keep other passengers from having to wait while you fish into your pocket for the right coins. When someone in front of you is slow getting onto the bus, be patient. You won't speed things up by pushing.

Subways, Trains

SIT ONLY ON YOUR PART OF THE SEAT and keep your books and packages on your lap, to yourself. If you're on an inside seat, say "Excuse me" when you're ready to leave, and again as you make your way through a crowd to the door.

ACTING LIKE A SHOW-OFF by talking loud and rough-housing is very annoying to the other passengers—and in some cities, bus drivers won't allow it. Better save this sort of fun for the playground.

SAVE THE OPERATOR'S NERVES and your neck by waiting until a vehicle has come to a full stop before getting off. Pushing, in an effort to get ahead, won't get you off any faster, so move along with the crowd and keep things pleasant.

WHEN YOU HAVE TO STAND, be sure you do it on your own feet, not some other passenger's. Never lean on someone who's seated. Hold on to a strap or the back of a seat to avoid being jolted against other passengers.

SUBWAY, ELEVATED, OR TRAIN PLATFORMS can be dangerous places, so don't play running or tussling games while waiting for trains. Never linger to play on a platform after leaving a subway train. It's not safe and can be very annoying to the other passengers.

*P*erhaps you won't ride in a taxicab alone very often, but it's a good idea to know how.

TAXI DRIVERS are usually very helpful men who want to make your ride pleasant. As you get into a cab, tell the driver where you want to go. He knows the city, so let him decide the route he'll take.

MOST DRIVERS LIKE TO TALK, and he's one stranger you needn't be afraid to talk to, because he really is not a stranger at all. The cab company has found out all about him and is sure that he's a reliable person before he's allowed to drive one of their cabs.

THE METER, which is to the driver's right in most cabs, shows the amount you owe. It ticks when the cab's motor is running, registering the amount due. This gets higher and higher as the miles roll by. Look at it just before you reach the end of your ride to see just how much you'll have to pay.

Auto Rides

TIPS to the driver are usually between twenty and fifty cents, depending on how long the ride was. This should be given to the driver when you pay your fare.

OTHER AUTO RIDES may be given you by teachers, friends, neighbors, or social workers. The rules of good manners—dos and don'ts shown here—are much the same for all auto rides:

DON'T ask too many questions of the driver. Don't complain and find fault with everything. Never make remarks about the age or condition of the car. Never jump up and down on the seats, lean on the driver's shoulders, or put your arms around his neck. Don't fuss or squabble with other riders. Never wipe your hands on the seats or windows. Keep candy and chewing gum off the upholstery and the floor.

DO make pleasant conversation. Answer questions promptly. If you enjoyed the ride, be sure to say so. When you come to the end of the ride, remember to look at the driver and say, "Thank you, Mrs. Smith."

At School

School can be fun because you're with your friends, sharing studies and games—and the lunch period is much like party refreshment time. For a perfect score in school manners, treat everyone as you'd like to be treated; act as you would at a party where you're trying to make a good impression.

TEACHERS ARE YOUR FRIENDS, so treat them in a friendly way if you want to enjoy your classes. Go along with their teaching methods instead of criticizing them.

CLASSROOM RULES are important because without them there would be no order, and your teacher couldn't make things interesting for you at all. So be a good sport and obey the rules.

THE TEACHER'S DESK is her personal property, so don't open it, either to satisfy your curiosity about what she keeps in it, or to try to find something you want.

NEVER BORROW anything from the teacher's desk without first asking permission. It is very rude to help yourself and then say, "Miss Jones, I took this from your desk. Is it all right?" Don't be surprised if she tells you frankly that it isn't all right.

"I'LL LEAVE YOU ON YOUR HONOR," the teacher will often say when she leaves the room for an errand. This means that she has confidence in you, and trusts you to behave just as well as if she were there to watch you. So when you're left on your honor, prove that you can be trusted by behaving well.

VISITORS and others who give programs at your school assembly should be treated exactly as you would your mother's guests at home. Once a program begins, give it your complete attention. Talking, giggling, whispering, or causing any other sort of disturbance during a program is very bad manners.

NEW STUDENTS coming into a school feel lost and lonely. Everything seems strange to them. That's your chance to be helpful. Show them around until they get on to where things are. Include them in games and other fun at recess. Talk to them at lunch time and ask them questions about the school they came from. A little kindness on your part makes their first days easier to take—and you will find that you've made some new friends.

COPYING ANSWERS from books or another student's paper during a test is not only bad manners—it's as dishonest as taking money from their pockets. Quizzes are given now and then to see how much you have learned, and when you copy your answers from your classmates, you aren't putting down what you know at all, but only what you've been able to take from someone else.

COPYING IS EASIER than learning, but students who know (and you surely want to be one of them) say that it's very exciting to learn and discover things for themselves. The things you learn are really yours. Keep your honesty polished during classes, exams, and when doing your homework.

THE LIBRARY is one place where quiet is appreciated, since most people there are reading. Avoid useless noise and lingering to chat with friends. Treat library books as carefully as if you'd borrowed them from a friend. Return them on time to give others a chance to read them too.

THE SCHOOL WASHROOM should be treated exactly as you would the bathroom in a friend's house. Avoid such things as throwing powdered soap on the floor, spilling ink in hand basins, throwing paper towels out the windows, or writing on the walls—even though you might see others doing these things.

GAMES AT SCHOOL should be played with the same enthusiasm as games with your neighborhood friends. Put zip into the game by entering into the spirit of it. Always try to win when playing team games, put your whole heart into winning for the team, but never be unfair to the other side. Big arguments about who won a point are out of place. A game is a game, not a war, so get all the fun you can out of it.

SCHOOL PARTIES are sometimes more fun than parties given at home since there is no host or hostess, but everyone works together to make it a success. Join in party plans willingly and always do your part to make it fun.

SCHOOL DANCES are fun too, especially if you dance with everyone instead of sticking closely to one girl or boy. It's the boys' place to get the refreshments for the girls, and a girl should eat her refreshments with the boy who has brought them to her.

ASK A BOY A FEW QUESTIONS about himself and he'll do his share of talking.

GIRLS SHOULD BE PLEASANT and considerate of a boy's feelings. If he's not a good dancer, show him how he can improve his style instead of sulking or criticizing.

WHEN A BOY is on the street with one or more girls, he walks on the curb side. This is the outside, nearest the street.

A BOY SHOULD WALK all the way to the front door with a girl he takes home and wait until she steps safely into the house. Leaving her on the corner or in front of her house is not correct, even in daylight.

Sunday School and Church

In our country, the two principal religious groups are Christian and Jewish. The Christian group is divided into Catholics and Protestants, and the Protestants are divided into many denominations. Since each church has different customs, not all Sunday schools are conducted in the same way. However, they are all important because it is there that you hear about religion and the things which make it important.

WHAT YOU LEARN is entirely up to you, as the teacher will never try to force you to learn or do anything. Sunday school is different from regular school because usually there are no examinations, you're not graded for your work, and you're not punished if you neglect your classes and do the wrong things.

YOUR TEACHERS are different from those at school, too. They don't teach school every day but are willing to give their time without pay because they're interested in helping young people to know and enjoy their religion.

THEY NEED YOUR HELP to make the classes a success, so when you're asked to read aloud, sing, or take part in any activity, do it promptly, cheerfully—and give it your best effort.

IF YOU'VE NEVER WORKED with a group, you don't know how much fun it can be. There's a glow of satisfaction that comes from a job well done, too. If your Sunday-school classes get together for projects that require work, be sure that you're right in there pitching.

WE GO TO CHURCH to join with others in prayer, to offer thanks for our blessings, and to ask for help in knowing and doing the things that are right. Your church is God's house, so it's natural to approach it in a spirit of reverence and a worshipful mood.

THE CLOTHES you wear to church should be in the very best condition. Your grooming should be your best, too. Keep your party clothes for parties because they don't belong in church, but do wear your very best street clothes. When it's raining, wear your rain clothes—but be sure they're neat and clean.

GET TO CHURCH at least a few minutes before the service is to begin. Stop talking as you approach the church door, and find your place quietly. When there's an usher on duty, take the place he offers you. Never make a fuss about where you're seated. Once you're there, stay put.

IF YOU ARRIVE while a prayer is being said, wait by the door until it's over and then go quietly to your place. When you're very late and the sermon has started, take the first seat in the back of the church until it's over, then move to the place you prefer, if there is room. Stay out of the aisles during services.

SIT QUIETLY. Don't bring games or books to play with during the service. Don't giggle, whisper, talk, or do anything which will disturb those around you.

WHEN LEAVING CHURCH, smile at your friends, but save the talk until you're outside. If your minister or priest is outside the church to greet you as you leave, always make a point of saying "Good morning."

A PERSON'S RELIGION is very important to him, so never criticize his ways or customs if they're not like yours. Should someone question your religion, don't get excited or annoyed. Be pleasant and say, "It's the way I was brought up, and I'm used to it." After that, change the subject pleasantly, as religion is something it's best not to argue about.

Movies, Theaters, Concerts

If there's one place you should enjoy yourself, it's at the movies. It's easy to forget that there are people around you when you're watching a thrilling story, but after all, they've come to enjoy the picture too, so don't lean on the back of the seat in front of you, or keep time to the music by tapping your foot on it.

THE BEST TIME to enter a movie, of course, is at an intermission, when lights are on and you can see where you're going. But if the theater is dark, wait in the back for a minute until your eyes adjust to the darkness. Then you can find a seat without stumbling or tripping over other people's feet.

WHEN THE SEATS you'd like are in the center of a row, say "Excuse me" to the person on the aisle seat and again as you pass those who've had to stand up to let you by.

GET THAT POPCORN or drink of water before you sit down—and save speaking to a friend you see halfway across the theater until after the show. Once you're seated, stay there.

DON'T BE A POPCORN DRIBBLER, gum snapper, or candy smearer. Keep your refreshments to yourself. Keep them off the floor and the empty seats.

USE A WHISPER when there's something you must say to your companion. Remember, there are people around you.

SOFT PEDAL YOUR LAUGHTER if it's inclined to be the loud variety. Put the brakes on if it's apt to run away with you. Laughing too loudly or too long can spoil the picture by interfering with the sound. Don't laugh out loud at serious parts in a movie, or when you see an unfamiliar costume. Applause, too, can keep others from hearing the sound track, so if you must clap, don't keep it up for long.

LEAVE A MOVIE as quietly as you came in, as others are still watching it. "Excuse me" shouldn't be forgotten when you're leaving the seat if someone must get up to let you out. Walk quietly up the aisle—and wait until you're outside the theater before you raise your voice in delight.

IF YOU'VE SEEN A MOVIE BEFORE, don't announce it in a loud voice—and don't spoil it for others by describing every scene just before it happens. Seeing a movie twice can be fun, as you see a lot of things you may have missed the first time.

POLITE THEATER BEHAVIOR is much like good movie manners. Fortunately you won't have to find a place in the dark, as most everyone gets to the theater before the play begins, so the lights are still on. Usually there are ushers to take you to your seat.

IF YOU'RE LATE, let the usher decide whether you should take your place right away or wait until there is a pause in the actors' lines. Late comers taking their places can be very distracting to actors on stage.

INTERMISSIONS are the times between the acts of a play. Most people like to leave their seats for a stroll through the lobby. This is the best time for getting a drink, going to the restroom or attending to anything else which might be on your mind.

CONCERT MANNERS are the same as for the theater, except that when you're late you do not take your seat until the selection being played or sung is over.

APPLAUSE MEANS A GREAT DEAL both to stage actors and concert performers, since by clapping, you show your enjoyment or appreciation. Usually you don't applaud during a play except at the end of an act or a scene. Concert applause is saved for the end of a selection, but be careful! Sometimes there are pauses which you might mistake for the end, so wait until you're sure that the music is over before you applaud. When in doubt, don't applaud until you see what the rest of the audience does.

Public Places

*M*anners in public places are no different from manners at home, except that they're used with lots of people you don't know. Good manners must be used wherever you happen to be if you want them to become part of your permanent equipment.

LAUGHING TOO LOUDLY, talking for the benefit of everyone within hearing, attracting attention by hurrying or pushing shows off your worst self. Be gay—but don't overdo the high spirits.

OFFICE BUILDINGS belong to grownups. Many different places of business are located in them and thousands of grownups spend a large part of each day there. So, when you're in one of these buildings, behave like a grownup.

DON'T SLIDE OR RUN across the marble floors to the elevator. Know which floor you want before you get into the car. When in doubt, look on the bulletin board or ask the elevator man.

PATIENCE is important when waiting for elevators. To signal for an elevator, press the button. Just once is enough. This flashes a signal in the car which lets the operator know where to stop.

TAKE YOUR TIME getting into the elevator. Pushing won't help matters, so go easy. Once in the elevator, step to the back of the car and face the door. Don't wriggle around while the car is in motion, it can be very annoying to those near you.

WHEN AN ELEVATOR IS FILLED, the operator usually holds his arm across the open door to indicate that he can't take any more passengers aboard. All elevators have been tested for safety loads and the operator knows exactly what these are. So when the operator says that the car is filled, don't try to get on anyway; be good-natured and wait for the next elevator.

MENTION THE FLOOR YOU WANT to the operator when you enter an elevator. "Excuse me" is the right thing to say when you have to move from the back of a crowded car to get out. Say it so that everyone can hear, but please don't holler. Such expressions as "Gang way," "Coming out," or "Let me off here" are not good manners. They sound demanding instead of courteous, so stick to a simple "Excuse me."

ESCALATORS are being installed in many buildings and stores, so brush up on your escalator manners.

WHEN GETTING ON, wait for a complete platform to appear. Step on it firmly. At the same time, take hold of the hand rail. Stand still and let the escalator do the work instead of running up or down the moving stairs.

AT A MUSEUM, remember that you're there to see the exhibitions and not to make an exhibition of yourself. If you're with a school group, don't talk too loudly or wander off by yourself. Never touch the displays. Follow the suggestions of the person in charge of the group.

THE SUPERMARKET is usually filled with many people you know. Marketing is part of everyday living and that's when good manners count.

TAKE REVOLVING DOORS easy. Never spin them so fast that others can't step into them and don't use them as a merry-go-round. Good door manners are largely a matter of being aware of other people.

APPROACHING A DOOR, remember that there are people behind you as well as in front. Take a quick look over your shoulder to see that there's no one right behind you before you let a door swing. Hold a door open for a person who's coming in as you're going out—and never push to get through a door first. Don't forget to say "Thank you" when someone holds a door for you. Boys always hold doors open for girls and grownups.

NEVER GRAB a pushcart when someone else is about to take it. There are plenty for everyone—and no one cart is better than any other.

DON'T TRY TO GET AHEAD of people who have waited at meat or special service counters before you. This goes for checking lines, too. Wait your turn.

WATCH WHERE YOU'RE GOING when pushing a cart. Be quick to roll it out of the way and say "Excuse me" or "I'm sorry" if you've been blocking traffic. "Excuse me" is also said when you want to get past someone else who may be blocking the aisle. Supermarket aisles are not raceways, either, so don't go roaring up and down.

KEEP YOUR TEMPER when other customers do something annoying. They mean no harm, but often have their minds on their shopping and not on you. You don't have to push and act sulky and rude in an effort to show your annoyance. Show your good manners instead by being patient.

NEVER PLAY TAG with friends you meet in the market. Don't pinch the soft loaves of bread, open the frosted-food bins, or handle the ice-cream cartons. And pestering your mother to buy something not on her shopping list is a sure way of annoying her.

Once your supermarket manners are super, you'll know how to behave in any crowded place.

At a Party

Some people seem to think that when you're invited to a party, all you have to do is to put on your best clothes and be there. Actually, anyone who accepts an invitation also accepts the responsibility for being a good guest.

THIS MEANS doing your best to make a party fun, not only for yourself, but for everyone there. You must be good-natured, a good sport about whatever happens, and pleasant to all guests. Do everything you can to help them have fun. It's a good idea to talk to those who seem to be standing by themselves and by this nice gesture, make them feel more at ease.

WHEN YOU HEAR that a friend is having a party, don't ask if you may come. It would be difficult for a friend to say no, but by inviting yourself you may be spoiling her plans. Wait to be invited. Many times your friends know more people than they can invite to one party, and will have different parties for different groups, such as their Sunday-school class, dancing-school friends, and their chums in the neighborhood. So don't feel hurt or left out if a friend doesn't invite you to one particular party. He's probably planning to ask you to one later on, with people who are your special friends.

ANSWER INVITATIONS promptly, so that your host or hostess can go ahead with party plans. More about invitations on page 27.

WHEN YOU GET TO THE PARTY, there will be someone at the door to greet you, usually your host or hostess and an older person. The first thing to do is to speak to the older person and then to your young friend. If you do not know the grownup, your host will introduce you right away. If it is a birthday party, be sure to add "Happy Birthday" to the greetings.

IF YOU'VE BROUGHT A PRESENT, this is the time to give it to your friend. A card on which you've written a greeting and your name should be included in the wrapped package to help the host or hostess keep track of who has given which presents.

YOU'LL PROBABLY KNOW most of the guests at the party, but if you're introduced to new people, "How do you do?" is the thing to say. For more about introductions turn to page 6.

IN PLAYING A GAME, if you're paired off with someone you don't like, be pleasant, regardless of how you feel. By the time the game is over, you'll probably like the guest much better.

JOIN WILLINGLY in any game suggested, even when it's not your favorite. Once you start playing, you'll probably have a good time. Avoid making too many suggestions

82

about games to play. Remember that the host or hostess has planned the games and too many suggestions on your part may spoil the party.

WHEN YOU WIN a prize, accept it with glee, but don't be a show-off. If you're the "booby," accept that as nicely as when you win.

REFRESHMENT TIME is often the high point of a party. Always show pleasure in anything that's served, but that doesn't mean dashing to the table as though you were starved, or pushing other guests aside in your eagerness to get there first. Don't overdo the enthusiasm.

NEVER OVERLOAD A PLATE, as it isn't attractive and makes you look very greedy. It is better to take less and return for a second helping if you want it. Things often spill from an overloaded plate, and then where are you?

HANDLE FOOD CAREFULLY to keep it off rugs, furniture, your clothes, and those of other guests. Milk, cocoa, Coke, and ice cream need special handling care, because the stains they leave are very hard to remove. Watch where you're going when carrying a plate of food, for a collision with another guest can make quite a mess.

WHEN YOU HAVE MORE ON YOUR PLATE than you can eat, never offer the leftovers to someone near you. Leave what you don't want on the plate without comment.

ACCIDENTS can happen to anyone, so if you have one, don't let it get you down. Of course, you'll feel bad, so say that you're sorry, do what you can to clean up, and then forget it. No one thinks that you did it on purpose, and too much talk about it can spoil everyone's fun. Don't treat an accident too lightly, either. Accidents are seldom funny, and to act as though you thought they were gives the impression that you're not really sorry or don't really care. Should someone spill something on you, be nice about it—treat him the way you'd like to be treated instead of making a big fuss about your dress.

THE TIME FOR A PARTY TO END is usually mentioned on the invitation, but even when it's not, you'll have no trouble knowing when to go home. When you begin to see guests getting their coats and saying good-by, you may be sure that it's time to leave.

NEVER LINGER after the others have gone unless you've been especially asked to do so. This is the time for getting the house back in order, and it's a job best done when there are no guests around.

MAKE YOUR GOOD-BY short and cheerful. "Thank you so much, Mrs. Smith. I had a wonderful time. Thanks, Bill—good-by," will do very nicely.

A RECEIVING LINE is something you should know about, even though you may not see one until you are much older. It is exactly what the name would seem to mean—a line made up of several hostesses, standing side by side, waiting to greet you and make you welcome to receptions of various kinds.

BE YOURSELF when your mother takes you calling—your pleasant self, that is. Don't run through the house where you're visiting, making noise and upsetting things as you go. Never open boxes, play with ornaments, or open desk drawers. Listen attentively when spoken to, and answer questions politely. This is the time to use what you've learned about conversation. Contribute to it when you have something interesting to say, but don't go on and on like a phonograph record.

IF REFRESHMENTS ARE SERVED, treat them as you would party refreshments.

Short Visits

*W*hen you go to a friend's house to play in the afternoon after school or in the evening to listen to the radio or watch TV, you're that friend's guest just as much as when you go to his party.

BEHAVE AS YOU WOULD in your own home, but remember that the things in the house are not yours, so don't be too free about using them. Always ask permission if there are things you'd especially like to do.

AVOID ASKING prying questions — and never look at papers or letters. They don't concern you. Treat furniture and everything else in a friend's house even more carefully than if it belonged to your family. Don't jump up and down on chairs or sofas. **MUDDY SHOES,** sticky hands, and wet raincoats can do much damage, so don't take them into a friend's house. Show your friend that you consider his things and his house important.

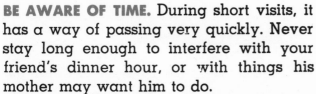

BE AWARE OF TIME. During short visits, it has a way of passing very quickly. Never stay long enough to interfere with your friend's dinner hour, or with things his mother may want him to do.

NEVER ASK FOR food or anything else you may see around the house—and no matter how much you may like something a friend has, don't tease, wheedle, or beg him to give it to you or exchange it for something of yours. When something is offered you, from food to a toy, take it without hesitation if you'd like to have it. Don't forget to say: "Thank you."

A SMALL PRESENT is nice to take when you visit a friend who is sick. Make it a book or a toy instead of candy or food, which he may not be allowed. And remember, it's for your friend, so don't play with it too much yourself. Visits to sick friends, by the way, should be kept shorter than your usual visits because they're supposed to rest.

When You're a House Guest

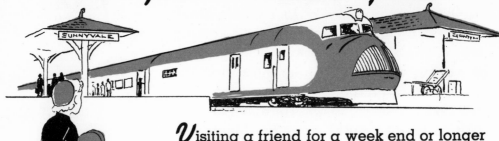

*V*isiting a friend for a week end or longer is a glorious thing to look forward to, and it's the very nicest way of getting to know a friend better.

WHEN YOU'RE INVITED for a house visit, answer as soon as possible. When nothing is said about the length of the visit, let your host or hostess know exactly when you're coming and about when you plan to leave. This way, everyone will know what to expect. Be sure to ask if this time is convenient, too, as you might be expected to stay a longer or shorter time.

CHECK YOUR SUITCASE to make sure that you have included toothbrush and paste, hairbrush, comb, pajamas or nightgown, bathrobe and slippers, vitamins (if you take them), and soap, if you use a special kind. Take letter paper, pen, ink, and stamps if you plan to stay long enough to write letters.

TAKE A SMALL GIFT to your friend's mother if you like. It's not a manners must, but a very thoughtful thing to do. A book, handkerchief, letter paper, candy, or something which you've made are all nice presents. It's extra thoughtful to take a small gift to your friend, too.

HOUSES are apt to be run different ways, so when you go visiting, you may find things nothing like your home. If you're surprised, either by the elegance or the simple quality of a house, don't make remarks such as, "I've never eaten in the kitchen before," or, "We wouldn't do it this way at home," or, "Gee, maids all over the place!" Take things the way you find them and enjoy being with your friend in his own surroundings. Never make unpleasant remarks about other people you meet in a house. Don't ask prying questions about members of the family who may seem to have something wrong with them.

BE KIND AND COURTEOUS to everyone you meet in a friend's house. Stand when an older person enters the room, and offer him the best chair in the room, even if it's the one on which you are sitting. Be your pleasant and charming self and everyone will enjoy having you as a guest.

THINK TWICE before you tell your friends things you've accidentally heard your mother and father saying about private family matters. You may think these things are very interesting, but telling them can lead to a lot of trouble. This is also a good rule to follow in telling other people anything you might overhear in your friend's house. Act as if you hadn't heard it, and everyone will be better off.

CONFORM to the rules of the household, even if they're different from home. If all the children must be in their rooms by a certain hour, see that you're in yours, too— even if it's earlier than your usual bedtime. Try to fit into the ways of the house without trouble. You'll be happier if you do.

BE AN EXPLORER when foods you've never tasted before are offered you. Try them before you say you don't care for any. If you don't like them, eat a small amount and leave the rest on your plate.

YOUR HOSTESS is not supposed to entertain you every minute, so find ways of entertaining yourself instead of being bored when there's nothing special on the program.

WHEN THERE ARE NO MAIDS in a house, you can do lots of things to help. Making your own bed and straightening your room are two good ways. If the children you're visiting do part of the housework, ask if you can do some, too. You'll have more fun if you take part in what's going on.

SOMETIMES IT'S EASIER for a hostess to do things without help, so don't insist upon helping or feel offended if your offer is not accepted.

DON'T TEASE household pets. Not only is it unkind, but it can be dangerous. Remember that to a dog or cat you are a stranger, so make friends gently.

DON'T MAKE THE BATHROOM your favorite parking place. The early-morning hours, when the men in the house are hurrying to work, is the wrong time to choose for playing in the bathtub. If you share a bathroom, ask your hostess what time of day is the best for bathing.

WHETHER YOU SHARE the bathroom with the rest of the family or have one to yourself, there's no getting away from the fact that you must leave it clean after using. Leave no cloths or bath towels on the floor or in the tub. The washcloth shouldn't be left in a wet ball, either.

ACCIDENTS which happen while you're visiting are treated like those which come about at any other time. Explain what's gone wrong, say that you're sorry, and do what you can to repair the damage. Of course, you know better than to try to hide something you've spilled or broken. No one will hold an accident against you, but everyone will know that there's something wrong with your manners if you try to pretend that it didn't happen.

BE SURE that your hostess knows when you plan to leave, and be ready to go when the time comes. If your hostess says, "I wish you could stay longer," don't take it as a signal to unpack your bags and settle down for another week. It's just her way of saying how much she enjoyed having you for the visit.

GOOD-BY SHOULD BE SHORT and cheerful. Don't hesitate to say how much you enjoyed everything, and "Thank you" for the visit, too.

A THANK-YOU NOTE should be written to your friend's mother in addition to having said your thanks when you left. It's nice to write to your friend at the same time. These notes should be written within one week. The sooner they're done, the better—and there's never an excuse for not writing them.

Now You Know— Or Do You?

By the time you come to this chapter, you will have learned a great many things about manners. Sometimes people feel that knowing what to say and do is all that is necessary. They excuse bad behavior by saying, "Oh, well—I know better." But knowing what's right is only part of having good manners. It's *doing* what you know that counts.

If you'd like to test your manners, check the questions below. Read each one carefully and answer it with a "yes" or a "no" written in the space beside the question. Then turn to page 94 to see how many of your answers are right. Give yourself 4 points for each right answer. Add up your score.

If it's 32 or below, there are parts of this book which you should read again. If it's between 76 and 88, you have **very good manners**—and if it's between 88 and 100, you'll probably grow up to be a diplomat, as your manners have already become a part of you.

Questions

1. Do you keep a prize you win at your own party? _____
2. Do you help yourself before passing food to a guest? _____
3. Should you ask a stranger into the house when you answer the door? _____
4. Do you mention a girl's name first when introducing her to a boy? _____
5. Is it polite to wipe your fingers on the napkin? _____
6. Should you say you don't like a present that's been given you? _____
7. Should you stand when a grownup enters the room? _____
8. Would you blame someone for something you did if you thought that no one would find out? _____
9. Is "Coming out" the right thing to say when you want to get out of a crowded elevator? _____

10. Is it a good idea to walk backward on the street? _____
11. Should you help new students find their way around school? _____
12. Do the knife and fork belong on the table when you pass your plate for a second helping? _____
13. Would you make remarks about things in a friend's house which are different from home? _____
14. Do you hurry onto a train ahead of others so that you can get a seat? _____
15. Do you tip a taxi driver? _____
16. Is it all right to tease a friend's dog when you're visiting? _____
17. Should you plan your parties with your mother? _____
18. Is it all right to copy from someone's paper during a test at school? _____
19. Should soup be cooled by stirring around? _____
20. Do you have to conform to household rules when visiting? _____
21. Should you ask personal questions if you want to know something about a friend? _____
22. Is it all right to act cross if a friend has an accident in your house? _____
23. Does a boy always walk on the inside when on the street with a girl? _____
24. Do you always have to put things in good order before returning them? _____
25. Are there any foods you can eat with your fingers? _____

ANSWERS TO QUESTIONS ON PAGES 92 AND 93.

1. No	6. No	11. Yes	16. No	21. No
2. No	7. Yes	12. No	17. Yes	22. No
3. No	8. No	13. No	18. No	23. No
4. Yes	9. No	14. No	19. No	24. Yes
5. Yes	10. No	15. Yes	20. Yes	25. Yes

Index